Web

Echeverrie

Enefa

2/28/2013

Web

The Spider and The Fly

Chukwuemeka Ekemezie

authorHOUSE®

AuthorHouse™
1663 Liberty Drive
Bloomington, IN 47403
www.authorhouse.com
Phone: 1-800-839-8640

Published by AuthorHouse   01/25/2013

ISBN: 978-1-4817-0763-3 (sc)
ISBN: 978-1-4817-0762-6 (e)

Library of Congress Control Number: 2013900938

DEDICATION

Only those close to you may excuse, and understand, the long hours not devoted to helping out with the chores of daily living. They alone see you toil away at some seemingly unproductive enterprise, and, yet, respectfully preserve your work-space, which may well have displaced their living space. Miraculously, they keep your manuscripts from coming to certain ruin, as scrap. Such has been the inestimable help given me by my family, as far as producing this book is concerned. And so I salute Dr. Vivian Ekemezie, my wife, and my children: Michael, Richard, and Allen.

FOREWORD

After almost 35 years of letting my scraggy thoughts lie fallow, I've finally decided to have other people take a peek at my scribbling, if they'd deign to. In my college years at University of Nigeria, Nsukka, I'd had some rag-tag poems displayed on overburdened, tawny boards in dank hallways that constantly bustled with a gaggle of students. Some of those poems even managed to wing their way to cottage campus magazines.

Sometimes, the posted or printed poems, in those pesky days, attracted only leery responses; other times, they were warmly, even reverently, received. But nothing by way of those measured responses spurred me on to seek publication or further exposure. Indeed, the late 80's and the early 80's constituted for me years of irresolute ferment, sometimes of unfettered poetic access.

And then the heat dissipated. The wind-mill went silent. What followed were arid years of indecision and lethargy. In-between, I lost some of my early writings, from having to make desultory living adjustments. Was there any point in penning ludicrous thoughts that were doomed to die at conception?

But now, this late emergence! A serendipitous encounter recently re-ignited the spark and made it possible for me to finally come forth with this little collection of plaid ruminations. Indeed, Salman Rushdie's words ring unmistakably true in relation to the raison d'etre for this collection of poems, " A poet's work is to name the unnamable, to point at frauds, to take sides, start arguments, shape the world, and stop it from going to sleep."

Dramatic events and some splendidly torrid currents of emotions and/or sensibilities may compel an artist, or a debutante, to write, even if in putative hues. An artist's writings, therefore, may sometimes rend a person's inner core, forcing both writer and reader to contemplate the contorted logic of the mind, and of the times. A writer is apt, ultimately, to engage in rhetorical or dialogic examination of historical or contemporaneous realities that may not always be palatable. As Robert Frost eloquently observes, "A poem begins as a lump in the throat, a sense of irony, homesickness, lovesickness."

Web, arguably, represents long-accrued lumps in my throat that must now be dislodged. Assuredly, other lumps will develop and demand forceful emesis. In any case, dislodgement of artistic lumps must happen first before any heed is paid to what the cognoscenti might think of the ensuing product. It is hoped that readers of this anthology will earnestly plumb what truths may lie beneath the verbiage, and not become encumbered by fealties to conventions and artistic traditions. I've endeavored, as best I can, to pose arguments through what I've lived, and seen others live.

Inherent in those life experiences are attempts to tease out, from ordinary pleasures and ironies of domestic life, some moral extensions, some unexpected, wrenching consequences, or some plain humor. The reader bears the burden of giving any imaginable amplitude to this collection. In effect, then, *Web* represents my attempt at uniting compressed thoughts with truth, startling pleasure, and existential jousts. Let the reader, therefore, be the judge. Here are the inelegant lumps of my life laid bare!

Chukwuemeka Ekemezie, PhD
Blaine, Minnesota
2013

Contents

Web

Listen more to things
    That make us stronger
In the heart,
And firmer in the leg.

Evil tongues
    Lure us into lurid thoughts
    And goad us to rank deeds.
    Like stray cotton-tufts,
We have drifted aimlessly.

    Hot, sly wisps of gossip
    Waft daily into the catacombs
Of our hearts
    Blurring our thinking.

BUT NOW:
Listen more to things
Of the soul—
Things that web us
Closely together.

Miscellaneous III

Under the burning sun,
Inside dinghy rooms,
From torn toilet-seats,
Voices compel attention . . .

Listen to big birds
Argue about death.
Watch their black wings
Span and measure
The breadth of human shame . . .

And men have courted fame
And men have treasured phlegm.

Watch big, black birds
Droop their wings
And hide among humans.
Humans are devalued,
Like torn drums.

People have courted fame-
Soared like angels,
And plummeted to shame.

Like guilty squirrels
You wash your hands of blame,
But blood can't cleanse blood-
Guilt begets guilt . . .

You who perfume decay
Only stay the rot for a while.
The wheels must turn . . .

Let none dare uproot the tree;
Let none overturn justice.

*   *   *

We waited calmly
Below the mountain,
Thinking you'd bring the boom.

But down you came
With shiny faces,
Faces sated with easement . . .
You didn't even have eyes for us.

Perhaps we'll have to stone again
To refocus your sight!

With pithy voices that name beatitudes,
But can't weep for our pain,
You jar in your noisy drone,
Lulling us to fitful sleep.

We await the cudgel;
We await the undertaker.

You who drive away the vultures-
What about the corpses?
What about the dead?

Sleep on, beloved:
Sleep on in death.
Yours is a sweeter state.

No more for you:
The mildewed blossoms;
No more:
The dagger of hunger.
Like one mortally wounded in war
You've bled to swanness,
Losing all your anger.

Let none drive off the vultures!
Life is sweeter in death . . .

*   *   *

Even if we bury anger now,
It will sprout again;
Even if we bury anger,
It will resurrect.
Let's now not inter justice
Let none uproot the tree . . .

Each time l pick up a word
To beat and tinker to sheenness,
Shadows smother it,
Deny it of timbre and mettle.
We can't well varnish the ugly;
We can't well garnish the dross.

Let no man color the truth:
Mirrors don't tell lies . . .

*   *   *

Our fat-crotched, thieving rulers
Drop vows
Casually,
Like soiled napkins.

*   *   *

People do court fame
But then lurch on to grime,
Relishing cocktails of shame.

Stares

Cockatrice-stares
Malevolent, pulverizing glares:
Aren't they the cinders
That char up our egos?
Fiery gorgons flicking snakehair;
Hypnotic vision: venom . . .

Who'd then brave the cave?
Who can retrieve the treasure
From tongue-lolling Medusas?

Hateful stares have burnt up our hearts
And riveted our feet.

Time The Leveller

To those who dispense
Justice in stilted terms,
Whose canons of law
Guillotine the poor,
To those appareled today
In dazzling damask-
Becapped in fine silk-
To you who pine
For opulence in crazed desperation,
Those who draw
Perfunctory applause
From bleary-eyed minions,
To you all who
Despise the flotsam of history,
I say, history itself is a capricious beast-
It can devour today's heroes!

Today you may be cocky and hearty,
But, at dawn, you could be BURIED
In the mud of shame.
I say, time
Is a terrible avenger.

After Work

After work in
Exotic pleasure dens,
Mounting refuse dumps
Reaffirm your type.
Nevertheless, vault over;
Then ape round a table
The white man: napkins,
Cutlery, desserts,
Wine and lime.
Home at last,
Smell of red wine
Will mingle marvelously
With the soporific
Fumes from fermenting
Refuse heaps-
Your knolls of shame.

Schizoid

Piety boils in you
As if cauldroned
Beyond 100c.
Your piety bubbles
And dazzles
The eye unschooled.

But anger in you incinerates
With laser intensity.
Your anger scathes
And befuddles your doters.

Sweet songs and bile,
Curses and benedictions,
Guffaws and tirades:
They blend so well in you.

How, with a flourish,
Your schizoid self
Contorts in throes of ire and guffaws!

Pedlars

There's a broad chasm
Between you and me;
Ricocheting silence gnaws at
My soul and your soul.

And you say to me:
The wall you've erected
Between us
Has ruined our friendship.
Your arrows of mischief
Have impaled
The trust we once shared.

And I say to you:
Your treachery
(for long sheathed beneath wry smiles)
Has thrust a knife
At the knot that once bound us.
Your red-hot knife of knavery
Has bled our love
To weariness.
We have become
Two crisscrossed fingers
Peddling accusations.

Pastiche

I

Life-patches,
Frescoes in chiaroscuro;
Weird butterfly-
Weightless like the wafer.

We seat in gnarled pews on Sundays-
With our minds
Punched from diverse sides:
There's no food at home now . . .
Why was he not in church today . . . ?
My neighbor smells horribly . . .
Be careful!

II

Despair gushes like a geyser,
Lifting up the limb to fend off a blow
But also paralyzing the soul.
We yawn—listlessly . . .

III

Look at her!
Legs crisscrossing
Scissors-like:
I see nothing,
I feel nothing.
I'm porcupine-thick.

IV

Out the door she hurtles,
Like some missile,
Shattering my peace
Stoking my pains.
I sigh like a forlorn traveler.
I feel floods of bile trundling
Down the corrugated pathway of yesterday's dreams.

V

Flatfooted
Accomplices of mammoth crimes!
We have stolen your peace.
We speak of our agony
And strike for our pains.
We have retrieved your mats
So you'd sleep
With us on the floor
Of your perdition . . .
Calloused hulks!

Public Health

Moments there are
When the mind
Clacks to a cranky halt.

And your limbs
Can't even stop your yawns,
Can't even lift the hand to the mouth.

But healing sprouts
Like cactus in the desert,
Directing our eyes to Calvary feat
And to the groans of our Loving Savior.

Hope pops up like the moon in winter,
Pointing the light
To weary hearts
Made giddy by much abuse.

At such moments
God casts the day down
Like a canopy.
And rolls out the night like a coverlet
To hide our nakedness
And sate every jaded nerve.

Masks

For each new face we meet,
We wear a different mask.

For each wry face,
We pull off some cynical leer.

The same dry laughter,
For each false caw we hear,

For each new gathering,
We sport a different garb.

We have a different mask
And a different smile;

A different face
And a different dress

For each new face we meet,
For each new country we adopt.

I Shall Be Glad

Anticipatory of the final parting,
I didn't know that love could be so searing
For (I must confess) I loved your supple garden.
For four years I bounded across your fields,
Browsing here and there,
Bathing in your gurgling river.
For four years, I frolicked among
Your dank, jaded books.
Nsukka, for four full years I felt
The towering presence of your hills,
Your cutting cold,
And your blighting sun.
Yet I shall be glad
For another visit
Among your hills
And your dog-eared books.

Like Guilt

Departing feet,
Receding shadows
Of treacherous friends . . .

Now that I leave Sokoto,
Now that I roll up
My sojourn here like a mat—
Chasing dust specks
Off moldy bric-a-brac,
Putting a futile shine on shoes pored-
Like a face poxed-
Now that I fold
My thread-bare clothes
(Torn here, tight there),
Let me cast one last look
At this one-windowed room,
This humid trap
That has hosted
Hordes of feet
And a medley of feelings.

Here dreams
Were squandered,
Trust abused,
And ribbons of friendship
Strung and clipped.

Let me take this last look
Before my departing feet
Would add to the dust
Settling here,
Like guilt.

To Uche Emole (Dateline: 21/7/83)

When I remember

Though a luckier farmer
Is the preferred owner
And though your piquant coyness
Has won his tender caress,
I still regard with envy
Your budding primrose beauty.
Yes, sometimes I'm envious—
Though I'm hardly bilious—
When I remember
That I can never
Tag my name on you,
Though my love is true.

Love Songs

I feel love like a pain.
I feel love like a torrid sore.
Coital heat has condensed to
Hard, unkind words.

We should dance naked
Kicking around our hearts . . .

We should hold hands tightly
Kissing non-human lips
Singing a dirge to fellowship.

Copulation for us all
Has yielded bastard breeds;
Love has spawned
Angry, loveless elves.

So let's form a circle
And dance round and round
The cold hearth.

You who feel love as a wound,
Come and join the ghoulish train,
Writhing and trembling in pain.

Rainfall

And to you we sing:
"Te Deum laudamus,
Te Deum maxima laudamus."

And in you we exult:
For these pelting drops
That now melt
Our wearied crustiness.

And truly we shiver:
In dread of this
Numbing cold . . .
Glory, glory, forever.

But we fear now
You mean to punish,
To lash and to scourge.

We thought a mere sprinkle
Could have done the deed . . .

Lest we all perish,
Lest the last walls crumble,
Spare us this inundation.

We never meant
To test your power;
We only asked for some soothing drops of rain.

Prodigal

We saw her depart
Clutching many bags
Of clothes and whoricraft.

Then we saw her creep back
In twilight dimness,
When tears no longer rack
And laughter effervesces to meanness . . .

See her now—a polyglot,
Blotched like an over-palmed naira note.

Now her skin
Is blistered sorely—
She coughs out ruddy phlegm only.

They say she's dying of
A strange disease.
Her breasts can no longer tease!
See her now in pains . . .

Desperado

Dear elephant,
Why squash
The helpless doe
Under your feet
Just so you can prove your feat?

The doe—admittedly your foe—
Should at least have leave
To browse and breed,
To nibble at fruit or grass,
Since your gigantic bulk
Ill—prepares you for
Such petty tasks.

The Hour Come And Gone

Tonight, let the moon not shake
Her waist in a facetious dance;
Let no light refract
From her crescent teeth.

Tonight in my sadness
I've peeled off restraint
As tears freely furrow my cheeks.

Tonight, I've seen futility
Waive gaily like a leaf,
Dancing in the frothing wind . . .

The hour has come and gone
And I was not there
I was not there!

Laugther

How we laugh at you,
Now that reckoning is due!
I saw your ego sag,
Like some tattered flag.

You look much like a whelp
As you huff and limp.
I see you've lost your fangs—
How blithely your life hangs!

In Jail

Should it please me,
I could journey eastwards
Where discontent festers like a sore.
Or I could sail to the west
Where plaints deafen the ear.
Or I could go northwards
Where tempers flash like cinder.

Yet incarceration dogs me
Whichever trail I tread.
I remain prisoner,
Not of brick nor of rod,
But of deep-rooted churnings
Inside the bowels of my mind.

Day by day
Long-fingered wisps of guilt
Chase one another up
The padded walls of my heart.

Silently

Now that doors
Are being shut to your face,
Now that whispers
Simmer in corners,
Smearing you with scorn;

Now that friends
(Like crazed, rabid dogs)
Have swarmed around the carcass,
Oblivious of the stink at large-

That is when
To wail **silently**.

Iron Forger

Kindler of my smithy
Inspirer of the tunes I hum,
You, my strident bard!
Watch henceforth
As I turn each scrap of thought
Into a tensile sword
As I practice in toddling patter
Each pedigreed tune
Which you've inspired.

Hermitage

People are like snails
Hidden in shells.
We flick out feelers:
We feel, touch, taste.
But we withdraw suddenly
Into our cold, hard
Shells of unrelatedness.

If You Should Know Me

If you should know me
The smile on your face
Would wilt, like a flower
Under the glare of the sun.

I do not want to be the snuff
That makes you cry.
I am the ringed heap
At your door
Waiting to sink my poisoned fangs
Into your heart, suddenly.

Would you please step into our dance-circle
Where we do not mean what we say?
Let's all play the ostrich!

There Are More Ways

Should I fume
And froth at mouth-corners
Because the poodle
I feed has bitten my finger?

I will dam the flow
Of my venom—
I will sheath the dagger.

We do not, because
The boa has taken refuge
In the hut, raze down the house.
There are more ways
Than one of tending
The boil nestling
In the groin.
There are other ways
Of letting out anger, I say!

A Droll Old Man

Yesterday

Walking along **Market Road**

I met a droll old man.

Eclectic and histrionic

He could tell many funny stories.

But he was a dipsomaniac:

Flabby sacs at eye-corners

Dark veins meshed on a wrinkled face.

He wielded the toxic bottle

With dexterous ease

Today

Ambling along **Market Road**

I edge near a milling crowd

Craning necks for a closer view.

Lying sprawled on the ground, spread-eagled,

Was the droll old man:

Now bereft of histrionics;

Inert, but tightly clutching

His half-drained bottle of beer.

They said he fell as he drank!

*Market Road is located in Aba, a major commercial town in Imo State, Nigeria.

Estranged

I saw it swoon—
Our blood-hued moon.
I saw it drop
And spatter us with blood.

I saw something else:
When the moon was to fall
And l strove to catch its pall,
Your hand thwarted me.

Whatever your reason might have been,
I know that l saw
Our moon-ball plunge
And splash red blood about.

Ever since then,
The ruddy stains of betrayal
Have smeared us with guilt.

Ever since that vision,
We have become two sheep
That stubbornly
Graze on separate fields.

Fervently Knocking

Lord, let me not be the stray one
That, loitering, begs for entrance
To your kingdom.

Not after I've been scourged!
Not after the labor on your yam-field.

These past moons
I bore witness to the peace
And the healing power of your Way.

Have not demons crumbled—at my word—
You nodding assent?
Has not satan fled,
His stronghold strafed,
Brick falling from brick (ashes all),
Marvelous deeds through your Word?

Will you now, for this child
Of an unguarded moment,
Turn me away
From your Kingdom?

Let the blood of Christ
Blot this single sin of mine.

To you, Nnamdi

As music from this red-eyed box
Vibrates in my insides
Strengthening my hand
Rustling my mind,
I remember you, Nnamdi
My never-failing friend.

You stood by me
As we heaved our pens
Across hostile sheets of paper.
Together, we strutted
Round the book-brimmed orchard
Garnering this fresh-dropped fruit
And fetching that dusty, hoary book.

You, Nnamdi, l greet,
Mindful of other campaigns
That should find us as comrades
Heaving, weaving, cobbling.

**For: Tunde Thompson
and Nduka Irabor** (July 4, 1984)

Aberrations

The languid march
Of time this July morning
Muffles the phrases
And the questions
With which l seek to
Come to terms with
The prodigious aberrations
Now sprouting like hideous brambles.

Let's not talk of those
Clamped behind bars
For sundry paltry offences.
Let's not even mention
Folks guilty of monumental complicity
(They're well out of it).

But let's moan for our
Kindred-men: the pen-bearers:
Those forlorn pair
Who now languish in jail
For daring to speak the truth.

Unsong

Leaves that quiver
In the wind-
What giant hand
Forces them to genuflect,
Bob, trundle, and then float?

Leaves malingering
Like a hopeless question:
Dry, blotched carcasses-
What sad fate
Impels them to plumb
Dusty streets, salaaming
Grioting and pinching?

These flighty leaves-
These dashed hopes-
These spindle-framed
Carters of leftovers-
Who will sing their song?

Will they really
burn or rot?
Or could they change, someday,
To some fleshly hope?

Our Country Is Full Of Cocks

Our country is full of cocks-
Brightly-plumed, debonair flirts,
Long-crested and flashy.

Like the cock,
Our men cluck
For the women
Who can't resist
The cozy chill
Of twinkling, sizzling parlors.

Our women pine
For sizzling wine,
In readiness for the hissing kilns
And the probing pylons.

How Can I Flail Arms In SOS

I want to scream words at you,
To brand them deeply on your mind.
I want to paint a tapestry with words
To pose riddles and curdle your blood.

I'd like to weave,
And tie knots,
To cleave
And to rupture,
To uncleave images
With ABCD only.

I want to tell you my name in silence.
Yes, to entomb silence
And resonate it with unutterable mysteries.

I want to snuff out life;
Yet l want to sing of rebirths
And of the rewards of love.

I want to use ordinary words to say
That a whit of kindness
Is all the potion we need.

I'd like even to disown my name
And assume your foliage.

But how can I embalm ABCD?
How can I proceed
To inter thoughts and feelings-
How can we do the necessary exchanges
And the needed scissions-
How can our dissimilar souls weld
When silence and violence
Rock our puny beings?

How can I flail
My arms in S.O.S-
How scream, how write . . . ?

He Died

Yesterday, fear
quickened our preparation:
Our child was churching!

To reassure ourselves-
Despite our fears-
We tasked the limbs
To clean the house
And scrub the floor.
We were determined
To feed every mouth
That entered our gate.

But today, it is another matter!
The food is ready,
The house clean, alright.

Yet it is not light-footed dancers
We are feting;
It is not those who sing
With laughter lighting up their faces.

Our food is being devoured
By some corpulent birds
Which have lost the voice for songs;
Which sit and stare
And wag their heads
From side to side,
Dipping craggy hands
Into our bowls of food.

Violence Of Age

Fiercely l fight
To keep the keel
Of my ship straight.
Blindly l grope
In a thicket of brambles . . .

The salt of my tears
Is testimony to the fears
Wringing one real dry,
Wringing one really dry.

My life has dilated
And taken unfamiliar paths
In maze inside maze,
In a confluence of indecisions.

But fiercely l fight
Amid shifting ground
Amid wind-slings
And blobs of scorn.

Not that we're all
Equitably appointed:
The violence of age
Afflicts our ill assorted lots.
Will the violets wither?
Or is there yet a shard of light?

Encounter

There
(Like a tremulous question)
We dithered about
On trembling legs,
Biting on apostate lips,
Dreading this other joust;
Inventories taken.

There
We mimed like idiots
Sputtering, stammering
Silently shouting,
Stirring dormant wells
Not speaking at all
Not speaking . . . at all.

Good Morning

There's some safety
In roaming freely.

Just say "**Good morning**"
"**How do you do?**"
And strut on.
Just shake chafed or flabby hands;
Shake, then scrape off accretions
Once backs are turned.

Too familiar thrusts like:
"**How's your family today?**"
"**How's the new car?**"
Are fence-breakers,
Grave—diggers.

They lure one on
Bit by bit
Bit by bit.
They lure one on to bare
One's heart to
A hate-whetted knife.

Friends, there's a wealth of safety
In being free as the wind!

The Spider and the Fly

The fly struts and hums.
The fly sings, happy, she may think,
Perching now and buzzing off again,
Thinking the world is hers alone.

The spider, too, is busy toiling
Laying wispy snares
In pulsating wind-paths,
Crouching, lion-like,
Waiting patiently
For his bumbling prey
To sing happily along.

Two Times Have I Bled

Two times
Have l bled,
Two times.
And your knife,
Honed to razor-sharpness,
By hate and rage,
Ripped open my flank,
Each time.

'Ohanku'
Water_hunt

Big cans
Small cans
Big buckets
Small buckets.
Preacher, dealer
Boy or girl
Man or woman
Carry your pail
And fan out-
At dawn or dusk-
In search of
Drops of water:
Drip drop drip.

Drops of brown water
Droplets of briny water.
When will they
Fill all the cans
All the buckets
All the chapped mouths?
When shall our
Thirst be slaked
In this drag of
Drip drop drip?

Ohanku was the neighborhood street in Aba where my childhood
memories were both formed and singed.

Stir Up Your Pot

Set your pot on fire
And stir up clotted clumps
From a memory befuddled.

Prod the brain once more
And rake up sundry
Bits of incident, talk, or thought.

Burnish the mind-mirror again
And be the sole witness
Of a mammoth throng of faces
Filing fuzzily by
Jesting, frowning, or cheering.

I say, stir up your pot again
And discover at least
How much you have
Marred your world
Or how much you have been
Maimed by your world.

"Genem"

She used to stand
Like a poplar,
With votive ferns
Declaiming her name
And prickles castigating in vain . . .

But time has taken its toll on her;
Time has bitten deeply on her once-elegant frame . . .
Who'd believe?

Genem, of fabulous fame,
Genem, of vaunted beauty
Is now such a hag—
A toothless, mirthless log,
With stumps for fingers,
And two gnarled lumps for breasts . . .

Time and wear
Have plagued **Genem** forever.

The Moody One

Friend—poet,
What cloistered life
You live:
In pensiveness
In penury
Brooding, scribbling
Brooding, scribbling
What many may not know;
Sulking over
Indefinable issues,
Shunning—when others do not-
The sunspots
That flay your
Naïve resolve.

Friend-poet,
Well may you be
Mirthless in visage
Though your soul
Flutters in reeling laughter
And your puny frame
Is racked with pulsating pain.

Well have I understood
Your pallid songs, your vacant stares.
You must spin sad notes
Though the world is merry.

You must pull a wry face
Though the day is brightly plumed
For you well know
That joy is a flower
That must crinkle,
And the sun must
Vacate his post
For sable night.

Samora Machel
October 19, 1986

What? Dead? Charred?
Petrel, Oh, petrel!
Mozambican dread,
Petal-bright, nectar-fresh!

What? CRUSHED?
And your songs all entombed,
With melodies unplucked?

These flighty birds-
Swift to flare and
DIS-INTE-GRATE-
Have impaled your lips
With steely flints.
They've gouged your eyes
And robbed us of light.

Oh, petrel ! So soon gone?
Samora, Samora!

Dry up, tear-ducts.
Dry up, tear-soaked land.
We are robbed of light;
We're limp with bile.

The Candle

Here is a frail, flickering
Candle at midnight.
Earth-moths are flirting,
With casual suspirations.

You and you:
Give the stub
A last puff
Just one last cough
From a heart feebly cranking.
At midnight
Eerie noises tingle and clang,
raising sensations of fear,

You and you:
That's your last flint
Slowly dying.
Disarray. Disuse. Abuse.
A Cyclic unraveling and tangling of jaded riddles!
Flames. Lurid séances.
Flames. Burning cinders.
Soiled counterpanes and napkins.
Memory coagulated, lolling languidly.

Yes, sorely your candle melts,
And the flower of innocence also wilts!

Prediction

Time will come
For this cauldron
To disgorge its murky contents.

Time would come
For this riddle
Bobbing at the banks of patience,
To unfurl like a morning glory.

And time would come
For this linnet-
Full of songs
But gagged with tongs-
To strut about
And limn its
Long-delayed monodies.

In short, there'd be
Time sufficient
To display your
Floral emergence.

Tear Drop

A tear
drops
And I cry my cry
In dire solitude.

A tear
falls,
And a part of me
Is wasted—
A part of my soul
slips
To the ground
And gathers
Sand, grit, and death.

Dialectics

*"Then flew one of the seraphims . . . having
a live coal . . . And he laid it upon my
mouth, and said . . . thine iniquity is taken
away . . . (Isaiah 6:6-7).*

*"And there appeared unto them cloven tongues
as of fire . . . (Acts 2: 3-4).*

Lumps of live coal
On my tongue;
Weights of burning coal
On my profane tongue
(for my lips
have spewed
all the murk
the heart can brew).

So place the fire
In my mouth.
Let my lips singe,
In shape for this binge-
To forge this linkage,
Stew the dialectics
Of coals, fires and pious ghosts.
(And how can man be ghost
Unless he dies?
How can man be clean
Except he burns?)

Link

Is there a link
Between the hunchback
And my clayey feet?

Should I sketch
Morbid vignettes
Of the tragic twists of life?

Should I—to gauge the plight of those who groan—
Feel the blotched tongues
In knocked-in jaws?

All around me I see
Eyes vacant like the desert,
I see gnarled human forms,
Scraggy hair and suppliant hands.

Is there kinship
Among
The hunchback, the beggar, and me?

Reeds Of Despair

When, with wanton vigor,
We squander our seminal fluids,
Does it not break our backs,
Deny us of those roaring flames
That formerly licked our throbbing loins?

What, with a searing zeal, we once undertook
Is now choked to an irresolute limpness
By reeds of despair and age.

When Pinned Thus

Your balls are taking
A cruel squeeze now,
And your dick can't even rise to kiss a cunt.
Your vagina festers from neglect and scorn,
Your breasts are as flabby as an overused flip-flop.
The wind tiptoes
To nudge the cobwebs
On your walls and rafters.
The wind whispers
One leaden word: loneliness.

Your wrinkles deepen, and
Depression entraps you.
Now you wear on your face
Lines of dejection,
As your life fizzles out.

So how can you wriggle out
When pinned thus?
You're only an ant
And can only muster a fart.

When pinned thus
By feathery, mammoth hands,
How can you escape
From the dagger
Lurking to pierce your heart?

Loneliness

I've seen loneliness
Darker than death,
Noisy in its leer
Snapping tree trunks
And smashing tinsel roofs.

Suddenly, the birds jerk into nervous songs,
Heightening old fears,
Feeding new ones.

I've felt idleness
As bitter as poison . . .
So weightless are the limbs
When the mind is heavy
With dubious feelings.
So helpless and listless are we
When we can't shake off
The web of fangled emotions.

So helpless and weightless
Do you feel now
Despite the hands that grasp yours,
And so lifeless are you,
Though you perceive hear-beats
Chiming with your heartbeat.

Draught

I'm sitting cussedly
As time needles
My wounded heart, haphazardly.

Nightmarish thoughts swirl about,
Buffeting the mind-reef
From tangent points:

"The manufacture project is stymied."
"That schooling dream is dead."
"The tree in my farm is stunted"
"Effort is vainly exerted."
"The peace is squandered."

As I survey
The carcasses of dreams,
I sigh like the sea breeze.

For life trudges on
Even as prime boughs
Drop with decay.

Channels Of Pain

Channels of pain . . .
A millstone of grief.

There was no avoiding
The spasm searing,
Hopes fading quickly
Like the tulip.

My puny attempt
To grasp a raft
Was soon thwarted
By swirling tides
Of pain, and more pain.

But then, God,
Crouching down,
Knitted me up again.

His salve was soothing
His voice cooing . . .

Though I could hear
Some rebuke in His voice,
His mighty hand
Had pulled me back
From the deep pit of death

Moon In The Eye

Hope you'd understand
Hope you'd understand.

I couldn't help much
With stumped hands
And clobbered feet.

I only have a moon
In each eye
And they glint
To cheer your sky.

Vermin

Time there was
When the skunk
Trapezed and skipped
Across manicured lawns.

Time there was
When the vulture
Was eulogized in tinctured songs,
With votaries enthralled.

But then came the gale,
And the once
Ambient terrains of ease
Are now such sickly plains
Of stumps and barbs.

What gaunt faces they now wear
Who yesterday were so sated!

SUDDENLY,
They scurry to dark corners
Like bats in the night,
Furtively turning their rabid necks.

Decision

How long have I manacled my own shadow?

Was the dragon I've feared all along
The echo of my own voice?

Today, I slew a lion ferocious.
I tore him
Limb from limb,
And it was all
In my mind!
Take the manacles off!

A Tease

A tease
Of the breeze
Lulls me into a trance

I dream that
My heart is scorched
In the bowels of a kiln.

String on, then, the music,
Compelling a wink
And a skunky shuffle.
It's no use to struggle.

Soar and Soar

Hatch wings
And soar
Above palm trees,
Elusive to the bowman's aim.

Take root
And bruise the land,
For your sturdy waist
Shall bear up strong arms
Waving gaily in the wind,
Courting a caress.

You, oh my soul,
Will not sway
To the foul-breathed draught.
Stubborn-willed,
You will
Bend your knees
And ululate
From the bowels of your being.

Brighter Than The Sun

In vain do shadows fall
To hide your radiant face.
Your bright and child-like face
Enshrouds dark secrets.
Your face is prettier than
The rising sun.

Smile for this child,
Who gropes
For knowledge hidden from ancient times.

Let your lamp
Glow brighter
Than this sun,
So that the crypt in which I walk
May brighten up;
That your gentle rays,
Like a woman's hand perfumed,
May yet caress my burdened mind.

Let your rays disperse
These evil clouds
That threaten to swallow me
Oh, my moon!

I Can Only Go Under And Forget

The flicker of
My neighbor's lamp
Pokes this eerie darkness.

I can only go under and forget:
In the cavern,
Where the pith has no bottom,
Where the others incessantly howl.

I dread the cold touch
Of your finger accusing,
Thumbing past and present failures.

Only yesterday
I drank your poison.
You'd appeared in disguise
As you did in Eden.
Like the grass-cutter
You came to me.

Slowly, you gnawed at my walls
Revealing my nakedness.
You pierced my feet with lies.

I believed you then, swooning
At the illusion of your promise.

Then I retraced my steps
When I met the humble Lamb.

Yet I'm disturbed,
As my neighbor
Burns his lamp still,
And these thoughts impale, like steel.

The Harmattan

A clear warning
We had of it.
The sobbing sky,
Suddenly drying his face,
Gave some crispy belch.

Then numbing gusts
Swept across the land
Cracking lips
Crackling fires.

It was so comforting
To roll about in bed
Lapping up mildewed
Freshness of the morning cold,
As the day turned on noisy hinges.

The ladies
Could no longer flaunt
Their piquant smiles,
Fearing their lips
might crack the more.

Time

Tick, tock, tick, it goes.
Fast and tumbling rolls the time.
Beats and pulses, bits of life.
Tides and markets roll and fold
So does my life; just for a while.

In The Fangled Land

Here in their Jerusalem
There's no respite yet.
The mind is roiled
By gnomic sensations.
My soul is winged,
Swift and throbbing,
Looking for some anchor, and probing.

Above the jumbled drone
Of the vicar's voice,
Moldy thoughts jar my mind.

Is this a bedlam?
Is this the clatter of a storm?
Will this surge of thunder
Yield salvation?

As l squirm in my seat,
The land lies inscrutable.

The choices are:
To savor the tarantula's sting
Or to embrace the Savior's loving embrace?

To Be Loved

To be loved
And yet to be thrust
Into the maelstrom!

Never cuddled in mother's bosom,
I am tormented by
Those who dared not look
Her in the face
When she was alive.

Now I prowl the streets,
Prey to human knavery.
I'm a skunk
Spat on;
I am a dog
Cudgeled.

There's no hiding place for me.
I'm some bat
Rattled in daylight.
But why do I wear scorn like a dirty garb?

Were mother to be here now
My fears would have been her tears.
She'd have shared
Her little corn with me, I know.

God's Riddle

Lord, we marvel
At this gift
Wrapped in cotton.

We watched as the seed
Was buried in the ground.
And then we counted
Beads of time.

Now its harvest time,
And we rejoice
At this delicate riddle
Wrapped in cotton.

I Will Not Take A Pinch

Let me not
Smell the fart
Of the he-goat!

I know her disguised steps,
For I've once plucked a poisoned pea
From her evil tree.

Palm-kernel is my food,
But I'll not crack it
With the baboon.
Else, I'll have my fingers
Cracked instead.

The goat and the yam
Are not brother and sister.
Therefore, I won't
Join in this dance.

Let me not
Small the fart
Of the he-goat, I say!

Trance

Exhausted from work one day
I fell into a trance.

In the filmy canvas of the roof
I saw a hairy, fiery spider
Weaving intricate filaments.

Step by step
His empire grew
Until it covered the whole roof.

His work done,
The old, wily spider
Strode majestically
To his throne,
Resting on elongated stilts.

Then a flustered
Little fly
Flung its body violently
On the wispy trap deployed.

She could barely struggle,
As every move caused her more trouble.

The spider was ready
To eat his prey.
Then I awoke,
And saw that I
Was the very fly!

Forgive

With my tongue
I harmed you gravely
Never peering in
To see the true
Color of your heart

With my eyes
I've scorched your dreams
Like grass burning in the harmattan.

I never gave you the chance
To unroll your frescoed banner
To state your own version
Of the matter.

Ever before your garbled song
Could escape from your throat,
I'd gagged you
With poultice.

I wrung the sun-bird's neck
Before it even chirped.
I rent the drums
Before their voices boomed.

But how wrong I was!

Your beauteous soul
Is the temple of peace,
Though rough-hewed
Your face may be.

Your songs are the timbrels
Of the jay-bird,
In the cool of the morning.

Your heart is refined
Far above rubies,
Filling all the world
With contagious mirth.

My true friend,
I can only say:
Forgive.

I Will Hear

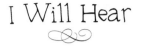

So when the last spark
Of fire is quenched;
When the hearth becomes cold;
When the children, sated,
Are happily ensconced in bed,
And goats begin to chew the cud;
When serenity hangs heavy like a curtain,
Then may the stars
Paint freckled images on your pearly teeth.

Strange events are happening tonight,
Budding around the cotton-tree.

Speak, then, to me in silence
And I will hear, my love!

Clay In The Sun

The mind recoils
From this invasion
Of lady wrens.

Now and then
They cluck,
Now and then
They cluck.

In my burrowed hole,
Craving for silence,
I have the clay ready.

But the buzz-fly
(I wonder where he came from)
Has perched on my nose.

Tired of all this, then,
For restful sleep I seek,
And wake later
To see my clay
Baked in the sun.

Bills and motions

The sneer
And the jeer
Soon dissolve the cheer
We'd hoisted before.

The panda
Prowls in circles,
Puffing hard
At his quarry.

The baboon
Shuffles and scurries,
Fighting off the lethal lunge of the cheetah.
All around is an arid plain,
Where the denizens know only so much pain.

It's fruitless
To hoist
The flag of freedom we'd dreamed about.

It's too early
To sculpt the figurines of justice.
Something has messed up the brew.
Something sinister has turned our song into a dirge.

The hyena in camouflage gab
Was chased away
By the fawning, "polished thief".

All we hear from this jaded breed
Is talk of "Something National Conference."
All they care about is their ration,
And not the Nigerian nation.

They pass bills and motions
To fill up their tills and work out their vile notions.
All they care about is their fart-filled bellies.

Temptation

Certain lurid thoughts
Creep into my heart
Stealthily, stealthily.

They refract voluptuous feet
Once nailed to the cross.

They make my leaden feet
Sink deeper in murk.

I turn like a fern
Here and there
Here and there,

Until, looking up to the cross,
I behold my Lord
Chiding, beckoning, shepherding.

Prayer

Lord, keep my mind
On you;
Keep my sight un-hooded.

Put a reign on my lips;
Prevent me from vain talk.

Hinder my feet
From hurtling down
The path to sin.

It hurts
To lose fellowship with you.

Nurses

They come
Wave after wave
Wave after wave-
Punctilious sentinels.

Each arch-hen and her brood
Dutifully mill and cluck
Mending a limb here
Binding a wound there.

Behind their façade of tenderness
Lies also a steely will
That could administer the barb
Whenever expedient.

What a clan!

Welts Of Pain

Yours is the song of pain,
Even though your petals petulantly unfurl.

You paint yourself in indigo hues
And preen your coiffures
To a dazzling sheen.

But I see through the
Skeined translucence
Of your grief.

You laugh and stomp
As one who should sail on the crest of the wind.
But I can feel the press
Of misery choking your
Delicately-hewn neck.

The peals of laughter
That ring out from your dainty voice
Also measure welts of
Pain inside your heart.

I can only say: "Ndoo"!

*"Ndoo" is Igbo word for "It's a pity!"

Many Thanks!

Lord, thank you for eyes
That can see the pelt of snow,
Hands that can cuddle a furry puppy
And a nose that can sniff the fresh, green grass.

Thank you for a voice that mimics the nightingale
Or sometimes offends like the crow's bumble.
I'm thrilled by the growl of angry clouds
By the roar of the raging sea.

Most pleasant is when, at the soft sandy beach, the cool wind
Caresses my cheeks and my bare torso.

I view the skyline on a clear bright night;
Marvel at the gorgeous way
You've decorated the stars
And made the moon wink a soothing glow.

I love the piquant smell of grass after rainfall,
And the cutting cold on wintry nights.
I'll be hopeless
Without the warmth of your love.
The fiery, grilling sun tones the earth at summertime,
But also shows how dreary hell could be,
If we fail to heed your heavenly call.

I love the gift of my wife,
Her smile and her gentle touch.
I love to see my children frolic and goof around.
It reminds me of my youthful days
And how your Grace and Providence
Have shielded me.

I love you, Jesus, for the beautiful world
You framed by your Word.

Etched in Gold

What is it that emblazons the sky?
What is that sweet scent
That sedates?
What is the swank melody
That softly tingles?

It is the radiance of your face.
The clap of your voice.
Your face ignites a red-hot glow in my heart.

You have a sure footing, and a gait,
That makes my heart beat faster and faster,
Faster and faster.
Your smile is a soothing balm,
Whenever it falls my way.

Your voice is a flute
That pierces the air
In lyrical tones.
The music of your voice
Is tonic to my frayed feelings.
Your eyes are lucid and bright,
Glowing like the Summer sun.

I feel your pain as my pain,
And your sigh as my sigh.
When you are glum,
I shed my leaves
Like a tree in the Fall.
Nevertheless, your frowns and creases are only momentary,
For you soon beam incandescent light,
Like the coy moon on a star-strewn night.

You are precious like a ruby-
The halo of joy around you
Holds me enthralled.

xx, I will etch your name
Upon the screens of my heart.
It is already etched in gold!
Go on! Make the world around you
Happy and bright,
Happy and brilliantly bright!

June 20, 2008

Love Bug

When it comes, love hits like a typhoon
Wrecking defenses,
And daubing febrile hearts with a fecal festoon.
Love is a sore eating up our senses.

My friend is a tendril [I still see her so] forking out to a
fangled social web.
I'm locked out of this nebulous nexus.
She makes no pretenses
Of her preferring the sizzle of 'professional colleagues'
To my cloy, constricted crib.

I'm 52; she's only 42.
How far apart we've drifted! It mattered little at first
Who was the more rusted knife.
But now, love is a flower shrunk and gnarled.

I make the motions of still loving her;
She grimaces inwardly each time I kiss her.
We have tepid sex.
We don't make love,
For love is not made like an artifact,
Or a concoction for a set purpose.

Her heart is lodged at a spot
Far removed from me;
My heart is fixed on her for whom I can't vouch.
"I'll always love you," I declare.
"I need variety," she says.

So take the word, 'love,' out of a life-time
Of solemn commitment, of inhabiting a room
With hidden closets.
Please take that word away!
Love is a Samurai sword adults wield like a toy,
Wreaking internal hurts.

Anger

Anger flares up between us,
Like desert fires,
And smothers us in guilt.

We trade accusations
And counter-accusations
That dredge up crusted feelings of hate.

What we've masqueraded as love
These sordid years
Has been some prurient leer:
Grimaces pulled behind each other's back,
Offenses stashed deeply in smoke-filled hearts,
Not seeking release,
Not seeking erasure-at all!

Dateline: November 28, 2012: Election Heat

There was a sudden darkening of the October sky.
A droopy cumulus threatened, then exploded, and rent,
Like a hastily cobbled bomb.
It was Sandy draping the land with its deathly pall,
Sending chills to the camps of two ardent foes.
From the soggy shores of New Jersey to the flooded streets
of New York, and across the snow-capped mountains of
West Virginia,
Folks scurried to safety, like rats chased out of their
tunnels by invasive bodies of spooky water.
Deep gutters of fear appeared on faces already
campaign-weary.
Anxious operatives wondered how Sandy might
malignantly wreck well-crafted plans.
Would Ohio be flattened by monstrous gales?
Or would that state nail the knave?
Would Florida become a red herring once more?
Or would Nevada teeter, and then seal the deal?
Colorado, Oh, Colorado!

Would numbers from Colorado clang the victory sounds?

Would they signal a giddy caper or a swan retreat?

Or would Sandy fizzle and burn out,

Like a hopeless dream?

Sandy did not fizzle out!

It had its sordid sorties, and then restively receded.

While Sandy's wrath raged, whites huddled and plotted

with Blacks/African Americans/Asian Americans/Hispanic

Americans/Fringe Americans,

Seeking to forge nebulous, tenuous coalitions,

Cleaving and uncleaving,

Heaving tall tales and peddling gossamer matter.

Barrack or Romney?

The rock or the hump?

How could the antelope outpace the fox?

Which of the two did Sandy grotesquely embrace, or

crush?